'WHY I AM NOT A PAINTER' AND OTHER POEMS

FRANK O'HARA was born in Baltimore, Maryland, in 1926, and grew up in Grafton, Massachusetts. He served in the US navy (1944-46) in the South Pacific, and attended the universities of Harvard and Michigan. In 1951 O'Hara settled in Manhattan, and soon became a central figure in a number of the city's artistic circles. For most of the fifteen years that he lived in New York he worked at the Museum of Modern Art, graduating from the front desk to become Associate Curator. He was a passionate advocate of Abstract Expressionist painters such as Willem de Kooning, Jackson Pollock, and Franz Kline. O'Hara wrote an enormous quantity of poetry, little of which was published during his lifetime, but which was much admired by friends such as John Ashbery, Kenneth Koch, James Schuyler, Fairfield Porter and Larry Rivers. He died on 25 July 1966, from injuries sustained in a beach-buggy accident on Fire Island. He is buried at Green River Cemetery, East Hampton, Long Island. His *Collected Poems* (edited by Donald Allen) was published in 1971, and won the National Book Award for Poetry.

MARK FORD was born in 1962. His publications include two collections of poetry, *Landlocked* (Chatto & Windus, 1992, 1998), and *Soft Sift* (Faber & Faber, 2001/Harcourt Brace, 2003); a critical biography of the French poet, playwright and novelist Raymond Roussel (*Raymond Roussel and the Republic of Dreams*, Faber & Faber, 2000/Cornell University Press, 2001); a 20,000 word interview with John Ashbery (Between the Lines, 2003) and a selection of the poetry of the New York School for Carcanet. Mark Ford is a regular contributor to the *Times Literary Supplement* and the *London Review of Books*. He teaches in the English department at University College London.

Also by Frank O'Hara

Poetry
A City Winter and Other Poems (1951)
Oranges, 12 Pastorals (1953)
Meditations in an Emergency (1957, 1967, 1996)
Second Avenue (1960)
Odes (1961)
Lunch Poems (1964)
Love Poems (Tentative Title) (1965)
In Memory of My Feelings: A Selection of Poems (1967)
The Collected Poems of Frank O'Hara (1971, 1995)
The Selected Poems of Frank O'Hara (1974, 1991, 1994)
Early Writing (1977)
Poems Retrieved (1977, 1996)
Poems with lithographs by Willem de Kooning (1989)
Biotherm with lithographs by Jim Dine, and essay by Bill Berkson (1990)
Hymns of St. Bridget & Other Writings by Bill Berkson and Frank O'Hara (2001)

Prose
Jackson Pollock (1959)
New Spanish Painting and Sculpture (1960)
Nakian (1966)
Art Chronicles 1954-1966 (1975, 1991)
Standing Still and Walking in New York (1975)
What's With Modern Art? Selected Short Reviews & Other Art Writings (1999)

Plays
Amorous Nightmares of Delay: Selected Plays (1995)

FRANK O'HARA

'Why I Am Not a Painter' and other poems

Edited by Mark Ford

CARCANET

First published in Great Britain in 2003 by
Carcanet Press Limited
Alliance House
Cross Street
Manchester
M2 7AQ

Copyright 1950, 1951, 1952, 1953, 1954, © 1955, 1956, 1957,
1958, 1959, 1960, 1961, 1962, 1963, 1964, 1965, 1966, 1967,
1968, 1969, 1970, 1971, 1973, 1991, 1994
by Maureen Granville-Smith, Administratrix of the
Estate of Frank O'Hara.
All rights reserved

Introduction and selection © 2003 Mark Ford
The right of Mark Ford to be recognised as the editor
of this book has been asserted by him
in accordance with the Copyright,
Designs and Patents Act of 1988

All rights reserved

A CIP catalogue record for this book is available
from the British Library

ISBN 1 85754 688 1

The publisher acknowledges financial assistance
from the Arts Council of England

Typeset in 10pt Palatino by Bryan Williamson, Frome
Printed and bound in England by SRP Ltd, Exeter

Contents

Introduction	7
Autobiographia Literaria	15
Poem (At night Chinamen jump)	16
Poem (The eager note on my door said "Call me,)	17
Memorial Day 1950	18
Les Étiquettes jaunes	20
A Pleasant Thought from Whitehead	21
The Critic	22
Poetry	23
Chez Jane	24
Blocks	25
Grand Central	26
Homosexuality	28
Meditations in an Emergency	29
Music	31
For Grace, After a Party	32
Poem (There I could never be a boy,)	33
To the Harbormaster	34
At the Old Place	35
My Heart	36
To the Film Industry in Crisis	37
Radio	39
Sleeping on the Wing	40
Returning	41
In Memory of My Feelings	42
A Step Away from Them	47
[It seems far away and gentle now]	49
Why I Am Not a Painter	50
Poem Read at Joan Mitchell's	51
John Button Birthday	54
Anxiety	56
Ode on Causality	57
A True Account of Talking to the Sun at Fire Island	59
To Gottfried Benn	62
The Day Lady Died	63
Adieu to Norman, Bon Jour to Joan and Jean-Paul	64
Joe's Jacket	66
You Are Gorgeous and I'm Coming	68
Poem (Hate is only one of many responses)	69

Personal Poem	70
Post the Lake Poets Ballad	71
Poem (Khrushchev is coming on the right day!)	72
Getting Up Ahead of Someone (Sun)	73
Hôtel Transylvanie	74
Poem (That's not a cross look it's a sign of life)	76
Avenue A	77
Steps	78
Ave Maria	80
Essay on Style	81
Poem (Lana Turner has collapsed!)	83
First Dances	84
Walking	85
Fantasy	86
Personism: A Manifesto	89
Select Bibliography	93

Introduction

The first edition of *The Collected Poems of Frank O'Hara* was published in 1971, five years after the poet's untimely death, at the age of forty, from injuries sustained in a dune buggy accident on Fire Island. While his many famous (and not so famous) friends and admirers had long been convinced of his genius, none, it seems, was quite prepared for the breathtaking scope and variety on display in this vast, slab-like tome. During his lifetime O'Hara published only a handful of slim volumes, of which by far the most popular and influential was *Lunch Poems*, issued by City Lights in 1964. Reviewers of these collections tended to praise the poems' freshness and casual charm, to complain about O'Hara's name dropping, and to treat him as an engaging minor poet: 'his amiable and gay lines,' observed one in a short notice of *Love Poems (Tentative Title)* in *The New York Review of Books* in 1966, 'are like streamers of crepe paper fluttering before an electric fan.' The *Collected Poems*, which comes in on my kitchen scales at around three and a half pounds and runs to over 550 pages, overturned once and for all the image of O'Hara as a poetic lightweight.

O'Hara was famous in his circle for composing 'any time, any place'. He would knock out poems in the midst of raucous parties, or in his lunch hours on demonstration typewriters in office equipment shops, or between customers while working on the front desk of the Museum of Modern Art. The poet James Schuyler recalls an occasion when he and Joe LeSueur began teasing O'Hara about his ability to produce poems on demand, at which 'Frank gave us a look—both hot and cold—got up, went into his bedroom and wrote "Sleeping on the Wing", a beauty, in a matter of minutes.' O'Hara loved rising to such challenges, as he loved collaborating with other poets and artists. Throughout his career he wrote much and quickly, and in a manner that allowed him to fuse the performative and the spontaneous, the poem's occasion and the poem itself. 'You just go on your nerve,' he explained in his hilarious mock-manifesto, 'Personism': 'If someone's chasing you down the street with a knife you just run, you don't turn around and shout, "Give it up! I was a track star for Mineola Prep."'

Speed was of the essence to O'Hara because he himself lived so fast. 'Is there speed enough?' he inquires in 'Sleeping on the Wing'— speed enough, that is, to finish the poem he has only a few minutes to write, but, more generally, to keep pace with events as they hectically unreel in O'Hara's world: the parties, the gossip, weekends at the Hamptons, the gallery openings, the latest Hollywood epic or Balanchine ballet, his love affairs, his many intense friendships which often turned into love affairs, then back into intense friendships, occasional glooms or bouts of anxiety, not to mention keeping up with 'what the poets / in Ghana are doing these days'.

To accommodate so much as it happened so quickly, he developed a poetic style that is immediate, nervously alert, mercurial, and evolved expansive open forms in which the excitements and banalities of city life jockey for one's attention, like faces in a crowd:

>   On
>   to Times Square, where the sign
>   blows smoke over my head, and higher
>   the waterfall pours lightly. A
>   Negro stands in a doorway with a
>   toothpick, languorously agitating.
>   A blonde chorus girl clicks: he
>   smiles and rubs his chin. Everything
>   suddenly honks: it is 12:40 of
>   a Thursday.
>   ('A Step Away from Them')

Such lines make us feel that poetry is not in opposition to time but somehow parallel to it. And the cumulative effect of so much casual experience and so many fleeting observations is to make his enormous oeuvre register as a kind of 'unrevised work-in-progress', to borrow a phrase from John Ashbery's introduction to the *Collected*. Poetry, O'Hara seems to be saying, is happening all the time, and an awareness of this is likely to be more exciting and liberating than whatever any single poem might tell us.

Although he knew his work was 'important', something in him disliked the idea of its assuming permanence too rapidly. He found more imaginatively congenial the concept of his manuscripts circulating through what he called 'a tremendous poetry nervous system', inspiring his numerous artist friends to new heights, or at least 'keep[ing] things humming'.

This kind of bohemianly nonchalant approach to the production and distribution of poetry ran directly counter to the academic orthodoxies of the late 1940s and early 1950s, when O'Hara began writing. New Critics such as Cleanth Brooks and Allen Tate had developed out of the writings of T.S. Eliot a template for the ideal poem, which they felt should be dry, serious, ironic, formally intricate, and morally responsible. It supposed a reader equally dry, serious and ironic, who would sigh knowingly at yet another set of illuminating fragments shored against one's ruin. O'Hara's poems, on the other hand, begin 'At night Chinamen jump / On Asia with a thump,' or are titled 'You Are Gorgeous and I'm Coming'. They do not celebrate the kind of 'Poetic insight' available in 'lean quarterlies and swarthy periodicals,' but 'you, / glorious Silver Screen, tragic Technicolor, amorous Cinemascope, / stretching Vistavision and startling Stereophonic Sound,' it is 'you, Motion Picture industry, / it's you I love!' If O'Hara has a moral to point, it tends to be of the sort one finds in the late poem 'Fantasy' (the last in this selection), which weaves together reflections on a variety of films with a conversation with a hung over Allen Ginsberg: 'never argue with the movies.' Unlike Ginsberg, O'Hara took little part or interest in the various poetry wars that raged in the 1960s—the struggles between the 'cooked' and the 'raw'—but his hip, glamorous, freewheeling self-celebrations both reflected and helped disseminate a new kind of confidence and daring in American poetry.

O'Hara was fortunate in meeting early in his career a number of like-minded poets: during his degree at Harvard, which he began in 1946 after a two-year stretch as a sonarman in the US Navy in the Pacific, he got to know Kenneth Koch and John Ashbery, and in the autumn of 1951, after he'd moved to New York, James Schuyler, Barbara Guest, Kenward Elmslie, and Edwin Denby. These loosely affiliated writers were dubbed 'The New York School of Poets' by the gallery director John Bernard Myers, who first published the work of many of them in a series of Tibor de Nagy pamphlets in the early 1950s, in the hope that some of the praise being lavished on the so-called 'New York School of Painters' would filter through to the poets as well. While they never formed a 'school' in any meaningful or programmatic sense, they did frequently exchange manuscripts, collaborate on poetic projects, and shared roughly similar tastes in literature, art, music, dance, and of course the movies.

O'Hara's early, pre-New York poetry exudes a brash, often comic self-confidence: 'And here I am,' he rejoices in 'Autobiographia Literaria', 'the / center of all beauty! / writing these poems! / Imagine!' O'Hara, as the poem's title asserts, was not in the least daunted by the traditions he sought to overturn or revitalise— indeed he gives the impression of rather relishing the battle. In a poem such as 'Memorial Day 1950' he self-consciously aligns himself with an eclectic range of experimental artists who inspire him to think with his 'bare hands and even with blood all over / them': Picasso, who made him 'tough and quick', Gertrude Stein, Max Ernst, Paul Klee, the Fathers of Dada, Auden (early, no doubt), Rimbaud, Pasternak, and—perhaps his most significant precursor—

Apollinaire ('I dress in oil cloth and read music / by Guillaume Apollinaire's clay candelabra'). For, like Apollinaire, O'Hara was the kind of writer who thrived on interactions with other artists in different media. His New York circle soon came to include sculptors, film-makers, dancers, musicians, novelists, playwrights, and, most importantly of all, painters, with many of whom—such as Jasper Johns, Franz Kline, Larry Rivers, and Joe Brainard—he collaborated on sets of lithographs, engravings, and cartoons.

Whatever the field, almost every artist who came into contact with O'Hara has paid tribute to his powers as a catalyst, and, in turn, much of the originality of his poetics derives from its openness to developments in the sister-arts, in particular in music and painting. On occasions he draws explicit attention to the processes of aesthetic interaction that stimulate his imagination:

> Well, I have my beautiful de Kooning
> to aspire to. I think it has an orange
> bed in it, more than the ear can hold.
>
> ('Radio')

In the much anthologised 'Why I Am Not a Painter' he develops a parable-like narrative out of the differences and similarities between the poet's and painter's creative methods. Despite its faux-naïf tone, the poem embodies a complex meditation on how art forms may mutually influence each other, but also evolve by exploring their own mediums in the most radical of ways. The poet pays a number of visits to the studio of the Abstract Expressionist painter Mike Goldberg, who is at work on a canvas that initially features the word SARDINES. Eventually the painting is finished and displayed to the poet:

> "Where's SARDINES?"
> All that's left is just
> letters, "It was too much," Mike says.
>
> But me? One day I am thinking of
> a color: orange. I write a line
> about orange. Pretty soon it is a
> whole page of words, not lines.
> Then another page. There should be
> so much more, not of orange, of
> words, of how terrible orange is
> and life. Days go by. It is even in
> prose, I am a real poet. My poem

> is finished and I haven't mentioned
> orange yet. It's twelve poems, I call
> it ORANGES. And one day in a gallery
> I see Mike's painting, called SARDINES.

The poem's symmetries are sophisticated and intriguing: Goldberg initially makes use of language to help him get his painting underway, but can only complete his canvas by focusing on the materiality of paint itself, while O'Hara, although motivated initially by a painterly thought of orange, actually writes his poem by breaking down language into its most basic units, 'words'. Neither refers to the sources of their inspiration in their finished works—except in their titles. At the same time the analogies the poem posits between the ways in which the two works were created vividly dramatise O'Hara's belief that all artists develop by experiencing art forms other than their own. What's more, the poem is both an illuminating compliment to Goldberg, and a touching embodiment of artistic friendship.

For certainly O'Hara found in the work of Abstract Expressionists such as Goldberg, de Kooning, Joan Mitchell, Helen Frankenthaler, Jackson Pollock, and Robert Rauschenberg both inspiration and example. In long poems such as 'In Memory of My Feelings', multiple, often contradictory figurations of the self are overlaid to create an epic sense of possibility and disorientation that in many ways resembles the unnerving experience of trying to make sense of an all-over Pollock canvas or a Rauschenberg mixed media composition. The imagery shifts fluidly from the violent to the bathetic, the sublime to the quotidian, and the endlessly resourceful 'transparent selves' O'Hara parades merely serve to illustrate the illusions of subjectivity. The poem's most resonant line, on the other hand, which was to be inscribed on his gravestone in Green River Cemetery, Long Island, energetically insists on the positive aspects of postmodern uncertainty: 'Grace / to be born and live as variously as possible.'

For O'Hara such variousness could be fully experienced only in New York, amid its 'crowds of intimacies' that press from all sides, its continual demands and soaring indifference. Like Whitman and Crane before him (to whom, along with William Carlos Williams, he pays fulsome tribute in 'Personism', proclaiming them even 'better than the movies'), O'Hara constructs an almost mythically enchanting vision of the city as the site of sexual and aesthetic liberation. His cityscapes tend to be as erotically charged as Whitman's or Crane's, though only occasionally, as in poems such as 'Grand Central' or 'Homosexuality', does he directly celebrate the pleasures of cruising.

He was also, of course, far too wised up to indulge in the kind of prophetic utopianism at which 'Song of Myself' and *The Bridge* at times aim, yet the New York that emerges in his poems is far more than a compelling backdrop to the ongoing drama of his *culte de moi*. Time and again we find him deliberately surrendering to the city, even if this involves denying the autonomy of his own thoughts:

> I was reflecting the other night meaning
> I was being reflected upon that Sheridan Square
> is remarkably beautiful
>
> ('Essay on Style')

Many of what he called his 'I do this, I do that' poems such as 'A Step Away from Them' or 'The Day Lady Died' involve a similar kind of full-hearted immersion in the rhythms of Manhattan, in the course of which anxieties and memories are evoked and dispersed by whatever happens to be happening on the streets:

> It's my lunch hour, so I go
> for a walk among the hum-colored
> cabs. First, down the sidewalk
> where laborers feed their dirty
> glistening torsos sandwiches
> and Coca-Cola, with yellow helmets
> on. They protect them from falling
> bricks, I guess . . .
>
> There are several Puerto
> Ricans on the avenue today, which
> makes it beautiful and warm. First
> Bunny died, then John Latouche,
> then Jackson Pollock.

In its oblique way 'A Step Away from Them' is an elegy for three of O'Hara's artist friends who had recently died: the poet Bunny or V.R. Lang (of cancer at the age of 32), the Broadway lyricist John Latouche, and Jackson Pollock, whose funeral took place on 15 August 1956, the day before this poem was written. Even such losses, however, are absorbed into the flux of city life, the imperatives of office hours which are only momentarily offset by the consumption of lunch and art:

> A glass of papaya juice
> and back to work. My heart is in my
> pocket, it is Poems by Pierre Reverdy.

There is no slipping the massive *Collected Poems of Frank O'Hara* into one's pocket, or even the large-formatted *Selected* published in 1974. This is a shame since O'Hara is, conceptually at least, such a portable poet, one whose work often seems most moving when read in snatches between other pleasures and duties. This thought somewhat consoles me for the absolutely ruthless nature of this selection, which runs so against the grain of O'Hara's aesthetic of 'bulk inclusion', as the poet Michael Hofmann once defined it. He himself was always somewhat leery of the whole business of choosing poems for publication: in 'Adieu to Norman, Bon Jour to Joan and Jean-Paul' he figures himself sifting through his manuscripts at a *Pensoroso*-ish midnight hour, for a possible Grove Press collection ('which they will probably not print'—they didn't):

> but it is good to be several floors up in the dead of night
> wondering if you are any good or not
> and the only decision you can make is that you did it

Let the poems, like the 'different bodies' that often inspired them, 'fall where they may, and they always do may', as he put it in 'Personism'. If for O'Hara the typewriter was to be treated 'as an intimate organ why not?', equally he wanted his poems to be more organic even than Whitman's leaves of grass, imagining them 'swell[ing] like pythons / the color of Aurora', instinct with 'sexual bliss'. As always, there's a jokey aspect to such fantasies, as there was to his description of the technical aspects of poetry as 'just common sense: if you're going to buy a pair of pants you want them to be tight enough so everyone will want to go to bed with you'. Nevertheless, there seems to me at least some justification for an edition of O'Hara one can carry easily about one's person, or flick through casually during a lunch hour—for poetry, as he points out in 'To Gottfried Benn':

> is not instruments
> that work at times
> then walk out on you
> laugh at you old
> get drunk on you young
> poetry's part of your self

MARK FORD

Autobiographia Literaria

When I was a child
I played by myself in a
corner of the schoolyard
all alone.

I hated dolls and I
hated games, animals were
not friendly and birds
flew away.

If anyone was looking
for me I hid behind a
tree and cried out "I am
an orphan."

And here I am, the
center of all beauty!
writing these poems!
Imagine!

Poem

At night Chinamen jump
on Asia with a thump

while in our willful way
we, in secret, play

affectionate games and bruise
our knees like China's shoes.

The birds push apples through
grass the moon turns blue,

these apples roll beneath
our buttocks like a heath

full of Chinese thrushes
flushed from China's bushes.

As we love at night
birds sing out of sight,

Chinese rhythms beat
through us in our heat,

the apples and the birds
move us like soft words,

we couple in the grace
of that mysterious race.

Poem

The eager note on my door said "Call me,
call when you get in!" so I quickly threw
a few tangerines into my overnight bag,
straightened my eyelids and shoulders, and

headed straight for the door. It was autumn
by the time I got around the corner, oh all
unwilling to be either pertinent or bemused, but
the leaves were brighter than grass on the sidewalk!

Funny, I thought, that the lights are on this late
and the hall door open; still up at this hour, a
champion jai-alai player like himself? Oh fie!
for shame! What a host, so zealous! And he was

there in the hall, flat on a sheet of blood that
ran down the stairs. I did appreciate it. There are few
hosts who so thoroughly prepare to greet a guest
only casually invited, and that several months ago.

Memorial Day 1950

Picasso made me tough and quick, and the world;
just as in a minute plane trees are knocked down
outside my window by a crew of creators.
Once he got his axe going everyone was upset
enough to fight for the last ditch and heap
of rubbish.
             Through all that surgery I thought
I had a lot to say, and named several last things
Gertrude Stein hadn't had time for; but then
the war was over, those things had survived
and even when you're scared art is no dictionary.
Max Ernst told us that.
                    How many trees and frying pans
I loved and lost! Guernica hollered look out!
but we were all busy hoping our eyes were talking
to Paul Klee. My mother and father asked me and
I told them from my tight blue pants we should
love only the stones, the sea, and heroic figures.
Wasted child! I'll club you on the shins! I
wasn't surprised when the older people entered
my cheap hotel room and broke my guitar and my can
of blue paint.
             At that time all of us began to think
with our bare hands and even with blood all over
them, we knew vertical from horizontal, we never
smeared anything except to find out how it lived.
Fathers of Dada! You carried shining erector sets
in your rough bony pockets, you were generous
and they were lovely as chewing gum or flowers!
Thank you!
           And those of us who thought poetry
was crap were throttled by Auden or Rimbaud
when, sent by some compulsive Juno, we tried
to play with collages or sprechstimme in their bed.
Poetry didn't tell me not to play with toys
but alone I could never have figured out that dolls
meant death.
            Our responsibilities did not begin
in dreams, though they began in bed. Love is first of all
a lesson in utility. I hear the sewage singing

underneath my bright white toilet seat and know
that somewhere sometime it will reach the sea:
gulls and swordfishes will find it richer than a river.
And airplanes are perfect mobiles, independent
of the breeze; crashing in flames they show us how
to be prodigal. O Boris Pasternak, it may be silly
to call to you, so tall in the Urals, but your voice
cleans our world, clearer to us than the hospital:
you sound above the factory's ambitious gargle.
Poetry is as useful as a machine!
                                          Look at my room.
Guitar strings hold up pictures. I don't need
a piano to sing, and naming things is only the intention
to make things. A locomotive is more melodious
than a cello. I dress in oil cloth and read music
by Guillaume Apollinaire's clay candelabra. Now
my father is dead and has found out you must look things
in the belly, not in the eye. If only he had listened
to the men who made us, hollering like stuck pigs!

Les Étiquettes jaunes

I picked up a leaf
today from the sidewalk.
This seems childish.

Leaf! you are so big!
How can you change
color, then just fall!

As if there were no
such thing as integrity!

You are too relaxed
to answer me. I am too
frightened to insist.

Leaf! don't be neurotic
like the small chameleon.

A Pleasant Thought from Whitehead

Here I am at my desk. The
light is bright enough
to read by it is a warm
friendly day I am feeling
assertive. I slip a few
poems into the pelican's
bill and he is off! out
the window into the blue!

The editor is delighted I
hear his clamor for more
but that is nothing. Ah!
reader! you open the page
my poems stare at you you
stare back, do you not? my
poems speak on the silver
of your eyes your eyes repeat
them to your lover's this
very night. Over your naked
shoulder the improving stars
read my poems and flash
then onward to a friend.

The eyes the poems of the
world are changed! Pelican!
you will read them too!

The Critic

I cannot possibly think of you
other than you are: the assassin

of my orchards. You lurk there
in the shadows, meting out

conversation like Eve's first
confusion between penises and

snakes. Oh be droll, be jolly
and be temperate! Do not

frighten me more than you
have to! I must live forever.

Poetry

The only way to be quiet
is to be quick, so I scare
you clumsily, or surprise
you with a stab. A praying
mantis knows time more
intimately than I and is
more casual. Crickets use
time for accompaniment to
innocent fidgeting. A zebra
races counterclockwise.
All this I desire. To
deepen you by my quickness
and delight as if you
were logical and proven,
but still be quiet as if
you would never leave me
and were the inexorable
product of my own time.

Chez Jane

The white chocolate jar full of petals
swills odds and ends around in a dizzying eye
of four o'clocks now and to come. The tiger,
marvellously striped and irritable, leaps
on the table and without disturbing a hair
of the flowers' breathless attention, pisses
into the pot, right down its delicate spout.
A whisper of steam goes up from that porcelain
urethra. "Saint-Saëns!" it seems to be whispering,
curling unerringly around the furry nuts
of the terrible puss, who is mentally flexing.
Ah be with me always, spirit of noisy
contemplation in the studio, the Garden
of Zoos, the eternally fixed afternoons!
There, while music scratches its scrofulous
stomach, the brute beast emerges and stands,
clear and careful, knowing always the exact peril
at this moment caressing his fangs with
a tongue given wholly to luxurious usages;
which only a moment before dropped aspirin
in this sunset of roses, and now throws a chair
in the air to aggravate the truly menacing.

Blocks

1

Yippee! she is shooting in the harbor! he is jumping
up to the maelstrom! she is leaning over the giant's
cart of tears which like a lava cone let fall to fly
from the cross-eyed tantrum-tousled ninth grader's
splayed fist is freezing on the cement! he is throwing
up his arms in heavenly desperation, spacious Y of his
tumultuous love-nerves flailing like poinsettia in
its own nailish storm against the glass door of the
cumulus which is withholding her from these divine
pastures she has filled with the flesh of men as stones!
O fatal eagerness!

2

O boy, their childhood was like so many oatmeal cookies.
I need you, you need me, yum, yum. Anon it became suddenly

3

like someone always losing something and never knowing what.
Always so. They were so fond of eating bread and butter and
sugar, they were slobs, the mice used to lick the floorboards
after they went to bed, rolling their light tails against
the rattling marbles of granulation. Vivo! the dextrose
those children consumed, lavished, smoked, in their knobby
candy bars. Such pimples! such hardons! such moody loves.
And thus they grew like giggling fir trees.

Grand Central

The wheels are inside me thundering.
They do not churn me, they are inside.
They were not oiled, they burn
with friction and out of my eyes
comes smoke. Then the enormous bullets
streak towards me with their black tracers
and bury themselves deep in my muscles.
They won't be taken out, I can still
move. Now I am going to lie down
like an expanse of marble floor
covered with commuters and information:
it is my vocation, you believe that,
don't you? I don't have an American
body, I have an anonymous body, though
you can get to love it, if you love
the corpses of the Renaissance; I am
reconstructed from a model of poetry,
you see, and this might be a horseless
carriage, it might be but it is not,
it is riddled with bullets, am I.
And if they are not thundering into me
they are thundering across me, on
the way to some devastated island
where they will eat waffles with the
other Americans of American persuasion.
On rainy days I ache as if a train
were about to arrive, I switch my tracks.

During the noon-hour rush a friend
of mine took a letter carrier across
the catwalk underneath the dome
behind the enormous (wheels! wheels!)
windows which are the roof of the sun
and knelt inside my cathedral, mine
through pain! and the thundering went on.
He unzipped the messenger's trousers
and relieved him of his missile, hands
on the messenger's dirty buttocks,

the smoking muzzle in his soft blue mouth.
That is one way of dominating the terminal,
but I have not done that. It will be
my blood, I think, that dominates the trains.

Homosexuality

So we are taking off our masks, are we, and keeping
our mouths shut? as if we'd been pierced by a glance!

The song of an old cow is not more full of judgment
than the vapor's which escape one's soul when one is sick;

so I pull the shadows around me like a puff
and crinkle my eyes as if at the most exquisite moment

of a very long opera, and then we are off!
without reproach and without hope that our delicate feet

will touch the earth again, let alone "very soon."
It is the law of my own voice I shall investigate.

I start like ice, my finger to my ear, my ear
to my heart, that proud cur at the garbage can

in the rain. It's wonderful to admire oneself
with complete candor, tallying up the merits of each

of the latrines. 14th Street is drunken and credulous,
53rd tries to tremble but is too at rest. The good

love a park and the inept a railway station,
and there are the divine ones who drag themselves up

and down the lengthening shadow of an Abyssinian head
in the dust, trailing their long elegant heels of hot air

crying to confuse the brave "It's a summer day,
and I want to be wanted more than anything else in the world."

Meditations in an Emergency

Am I to become profligate as if I were a blonde? Or religious as if I were French?

Each time my heart is broken it makes me feel more adventurous (and how the same names keep recurring on that interminable list!), but one of these days there'll be nothing left with which to venture forth.

Why should I share you? Why don't you get rid of someone else for a change?

I am the least difficult of men. All I want is boundless love.

Even trees understand me! Good heavens, I lie under them, too, don't I? I'm just like a pile of leaves.

However, I have never clogged myself with the praises of pastoral life, nor with nostalgia for an innocent past of perverted acts in pastures. No. One need never leave the confines of New York to get all the greenery one wishes—I can't even enjoy a blade of grass unless I know there's a subway handy, or a record store or some other sign that people do not totally *regret* life. It is more important to affirm the least sincere; the clouds get enough attention as it is and even they continue to pass. Do they know what they're missing? Uh huh.

My eyes are vague blue, like the sky, and change all the time; they are indiscriminate but fleeting, entirely specific and disloyal, so that no one trusts me. I am always looking away. Or again at something after it has given me up. It makes me restless and that makes me unhappy, but I cannot keep them still. If only I had grey, green, black, brown, yellow eyes; I would stay at home and do something. It's not that I'm curious. On the contrary, I am bored but it's my duty to be attentive, I am needed by things as the sky must be above the earth. And lately, so great has *their* anxiety become, I can spare myself little sleep.

Now there is only one man I love to kiss when he is unshaven. Heterosexuality! you are inexorably approaching. (How discourage her?)

St. Serapion, I wrap myself in the robes of your whiteness which is like midnight in Dostoevsky. How am I to become a legend, my dear? I've tried love, but that hides you in the bosom of another and I am always springing forth from it like the lotus—the ecstasy of always bursting forth! (but one must not be distracted by it!) or like a hyacinth, "to keep the filth of life away," yes, there, even in the heart, where the filth is pumped in and slanders and pollutes and determines. I will my will, though I may become famous for a mysterious vacancy in that department, that greenhouse.

Destroy yourself, if you don't know!

It is easy to be beautiful; it is difficult to appear so. I admire you, beloved, for the trap you've set. It's like a final chapter no one reads because the plot is over.

"Fanny Brown is run away—scampered off with a Cornet of Horse; I do love that little Minx, & hope She may be happy, tho' She has vexed me by this Exploit a little too.—Poor silly Cecchina! or F:B: as we used to call her.—I wish She had a good Whipping and 10,000 pounds."—Mrs. Thrale.

I've got to get out of here. I choose a piece of shawl and my dirtiest suntans. I'll be back, I'll re-emerge, defeated, from the valley; you don't want me to go where you go, so I go where you don't want me to. It's only afternoon, there's a lot ahead. There won't be any mail downstairs. Turning, I spit in the lock and the knob turns.

Music

     If I rest for a moment near The Equestrian
pausing for a liver sausage sandwich in the Mayflower Shoppe,
that angel seems to be leading the horse into Bergdorf's
and I am naked as a table cloth, my nerves humming.
Close to the fear of war and the stars which have disappeared.
I have in my hands only 35¢, it's so meaningless to eat!
and gusts of water spray over the basins of leaves
like the hammers of a glass pianoforte. If I seem to you
to have lavender lips under the leaves of the world,
     I must tighten my belt.
It's like a locomotive on the march, the season
    of distress and clarity
and my door is open to the evenings of midwinter's
lightly falling snow over the newspapers.
Clasp me in your handkerchief like a tear, trumpet
of early afternoon! in the foggy autumn.
As they're putting up the Christmas trees on Park Avenue
I shall see my daydreams walking by with dogs in blankets,
put to some use before all those colored lights come on!
     But no more fountains and no more rain,
     and the stores stay open terribly late.

For Grace, After a Party

    You do not always know what I am feeling.
Last night in the warm spring air while I was
blazing my tirade against someone who doesn't
interest
         me, it was love for you that set me
afire,
    and isn't it odd? for in rooms full of
strangers my most tender feelings
                   writhe and
bear the fruit of screaming. Put out your hand,
isn't there
         an ashtray, suddenly, there? beside
the bed? And someone you love enters the room
and says wouldn't
            you like the eggs a little
different today?
            And when they arrive they are
just plain scrambled eggs and the warm weather
is holding.

Poem
to James Schuyler

There I could never be a boy,
though I rode like a god when the horse reared.
At a cry from mother I fell to my knees!
there I fell, clumsy and sick and good,
though I bloomed on the back of a frightened black mare
who had leaped windily at the start of a leaf
and she never threw me.

I had a quick heart
and my thighs clutched her back.
I loved her fright, which was against me
into the air! and the diamond white of her forelock
which seemed to smart with thoughts as my heart smarted with life!
and she'd toss her head with the pain
and paw the air and champ the bit, as if I were Endymion
and she, moonlike, hated to love me.

All things are tragic
when a mother watches!
and she wishes upon herself
the random fears of a scarlet soul, as it breathes in and out
and nothing chokes, or breaks from triumph to triumph!

I knew her but I could not be a boy,
for in the billowing air I was fleet and green
riding blackly through the ethereal night
towards men's words which I gracefully understood,

and it was given to me
as the soul is given the hands
to hold the ribbons of life!
as miles streak by beneath the moon's sharp hooves
and I have mastered the speed and strength which is the armor of the world.

To the Harbormaster

I wanted to be sure to reach you;
though my ship was on the way it got caught
in some moorings. I am always tying up
and then deciding to depart. In storms and
at sunset, with the metallic coils of the tide
around my fathomless arms, I am unable
to understand the forms of my vanity
or I am hard alee with my Polish rudder
in my hand and the sun sinking. To
you I offer my hull and the tattered cordage
of my will. The terrible channels where
the wind drives me against the brown lips
of the reeds are not all behind me. Yet
I trust the sanity of my vessel; and
if it sinks, it may well be in answer
to the reasoning of the eternal voices,
the waves which have kept me from reaching you.

At the Old Place

Joe is restless and so am I, so restless.
Button's buddy lips frame "L G T TH O P?"
across the bar. "Yes!" I cry, for dancing's
my soul delight. (Feet! feet!) "Come on!"

Through the streets we skip like swallows.
Howard malingers. (Come on, Howard.) Ashes
malingers. (Come on, J.A.) Dick malingers.
(Come on, Dick.) Alvin darts ahead. (Wait up,
Alvin.) Jack, Earl and Someone don't come.

Down the dark stairs drifts the steaming cha-
cha-cha. Through the urine and smoke we charge
to the floor. Wrapped in Ashes' arms I glide.
(It's heaven!) Button lindys with me. (It's
heaven!) Joe's two-steps, too, are incredible,
and then a fast rhumba with Alvin, like skipping
on toothpicks. And the interminable intermissions,

we have them. Jack, Earl and Someone drift
guiltily in. "I knew they were gay
the minute I laid eyes on them!" screams John.
How ashamed they are of us!   we hope.

My Heart

I'm not going to cry all the time
nor shall I laugh all the time,
I don't prefer one "strain" to another.
I'd have the immediacy of a bad movie,
not just a sleeper, but also the big,
overproduced first-run kind. I want to be
at least as alive as the vulgar. And if
some aficionado of my mess says "That's
not like Frank!", all to the good! I
don't wear brown and grey suits all the time,
do I? No. I wear workshirts to the opera,
often. I want my feet to be bare,
I want my face to be shaven, and my heart—
you can't plan on the heart, but
the better part of it, my poetry, is open.

To the Film Industry in Crisis

Not you, lean quarterlies and swarthy periodicals
with your studious incursions toward the pomposity of ants,
nor you, experimental theatre in which Emotive Fruition
is wedding Poetic Insight perpetually, not you,
promenading Grand Opera, obvious as an ear (though you
are close to my heart), but you, Motion Picture Industry,
it's you I love!

In times of crisis, we must all decide again and again whom we love.
And give credit where it's due: not to my starched nurse, who taught me
how to be bad and not bad rather than good (and has lately availed
herself of this information), not to the Catholic Church
which is at best an oversolemn introduction to cosmic entertainment,
not to the American Legion, which hates everybody, but to you,
glorious Silver Screen, tragic Technicolor, amorous Cinemascope,
stretching Vistavision and startling Stereophonic Sound, with all
your heavenly dimensions and reverberations and iconoclasms! To
Richard Barthelmess as the "tol'able" boy barefoot and in pants,
Jeanette MacDonald of the flaming hair and lips and long, long neck,
Sue Carroll as she sits for eternity on the damaged fender of a car
and smiles, Ginger Rogers with her pageboy bob like a sausage
on her shuffling shoulders, peach-melba-voiced Fred Astaire of the feet,
Eric von Stroheim, the seducer of mountain-climbers' gasping spouses,
the Tarzans, each and every one of you (I cannot bring myself to prefer
Johnny Weissmuller to Lex Barker, I cannot!), Mae West in a furry sled,
her bordello radiance and bland remarks, Rudolph Valentino of the moon,
its crushing passions, and moonlike, too, the gentle Norma Shearer,
Miriam Hopkins dropping her champagne glass off Joel McCrea's yacht
and crying into the dappled sea, Clark Gable rescuing Gene Tierney
from Russia and Allan Jones rescuing Kitty Carlisle from Harpo Marx,
Cornel Wilde coughing blood on the piano keys while Merle Oberon berates,
Marilyn Monroe in her little spike heels reeling through Niagara Falls,
Joseph Cotten puzzling and Orson Welles puzzled and Dolores Del Rio
eating orchids for lunch and breaking mirrors, Gloria Swanson reclining,
and Jean Harlow reclining and wiggling, and Alice Faye reclining
and wiggling and singing, Myrna Loy being calm and wise, William Powell
in his stunning urbanity, Elizabeth Taylor blossoming, yes, to you

and to all you others, the great, the near-great, the featured, the extras
who pass quickly and return in dreams saying your one or two lines,
my love!
Long may you illumine space with your marvellous appearances, delays
and enunciations, and may the money of the world glitteringly cover you
as you rest after a long day under the kleig lights with your faces
in packs for our edification, the way the clouds come often at night
but the heavens operate on the star system. It is a divine precedent
you perpetuate! Roll on, reels of celluloid, as the great earth rolls on!

Radio

Why do you play such dreary music
on Saturday afternoon, when tired
mortally tired I long for a little
reminder of immortal energy?
                            All
week long while I trudge fatiguingly
from desk to desk in the museum
you spill your miracles of Grieg
and Honegger on shut-ins.
                          Am I not
shut in too, and after a week
of work don't I deserve Prokofieff?

Well, I have my beautiful de Kooning
to aspire to. I think it has an orange
bed in it, more than the ear can hold.

Sleeping on the Wing

Perhaps it is to avoid some great sadness,
as in a Restoration tragedy the hero cries "Sleep!
O for a long sound sleep and so forget it!"
that one flies, soaring above the shoreless city,
veering upward from the pavement as a pigeon
does when a car honks or a door slams, the door
of dreams, life perpetuated in parti-colored loves
and beautiful lies in all different languages.

Fear drops away too, like the cement, and you
are over the Atlantic. Where is Spain? where is
who? The Civil War was fought to free the slaves,
was it? A sudden down-draught reminds you of gravity
and your position in respect to human love. But
here is where the gods are, speculating, bemused.
Once you are helpless, you are free, can you believe
that? Never to waken to the sad struggle of a face?
to travel always over some impersonal vastness,
to be out of, forever, neither in nor for!

The eyes roll asleep as if turned by the wind
and the lids flutter open slightly like a wing.
The world is an iceberg, so much is invisible!
and was and is, and yet the form, it may be sleeping
too. Those features etched in the ice of someone
loved who died, you are a sculptor dreaming of space
and speed, your hand alone could have done this.
Curiosity, the passionate hand of desire. Dead,
or sleeping? Is there speed enough? And, swooping,
you relinquish all that you have made your own,
the kingdom of your self sailing, for you must awake
and breathe your warmth in this beloved image
whether it's dead or merely disappearing,
as space is disappearing and your singularity.

Returning

Coming down the ladder
you can hardly remember the plane was like a rabbit
                      the air above the clouds
                          that settling into the earth
                was like diving onto the sea on your belly,
there are so many similarities you have forgotten.

Well, there are a lot of things you haven't forgotten,
walking through the waiting room you know you should go
to bed with everyone who looks at you because the war's not over,
no assurance yet that desire's an exaggeration
and you don't want anyone to turn out to be a ruined city, do you?

As Marilyn Monroe says, it's a responsibility being a sexual symbol,
and as everyone says, it's the property of a symbol to be sexual.
Who's confused? Dead citizen or survivor, it's only your cock or your ass.
They do what they can in gardens and parks,
                      in subway stations and latrines,
as boyscouts rub sticks together who've read the manual,
                      know what's expected of death.

In Memory of My Feelings
To Grace Hartigan

1

My quietness has a man in it, he is transparent
and he carries me quietly, like a gondola, through the streets.
He has several likenesses, like stars and years, like numerals.

My quietness has a number of naked selves,
so many pistols I have borrowed to protect myselves
from creatures who too readily recognize my weapons
and have murder in their heart!
       though in winter
they are warm as roses, in the desert
taste of chilled anisette.
     At times, withdrawn,
I rise into the cool skies
and gaze on at the imponderable world with the simple identification
of my colleagues, the mountains. Manfred climbs to my nape,
speaks, but I do not hear him,
       I'm too blue.
An elephant takes up his trumpet,
money flutters from the windows of cries, silk stretching its mirror
across shoulder blades. A gun is "fired."
        One of me rushes
to window #13 and one of me raises his whip and one of me
flutters up from the center of the track amidst the pink flamingoes,
and underneath their hooves as they round the last turn my lips
are scarred and brown, brushed by tails, masked in dirt's lust,
definition, open mouths gasping for the cries of the bettors for the lungs
of earth.
   So many of my transparencies could not resist the race!
Terror in earth, dried mushrooms, pink feathers, tickets,
a flaking moon drifting across the muddied teeth,
the imperceptible moan of covered breathing,
        love of the serpent!
I am underneath its leaves as the hunter crackles and pants
and bursts, as the barrage balloon drifts behind a cloud
and animal death whips out its flashlight,
       whistling
and slipping the glove off the trigger hand. The serpent's eyes

redden at sight of those thorny fingernails, he is so smooth!
                              My transparent selves
flail about like vipers in a pail, writhing and hissing
without panic, with a certain justice of response
and presently the aquiline serpent comes to resemble the Medusa.

2

The dead hunting
and the alive, ahunted.
                    My father, my uncle,
my grand-uncle and the several aunts. My
grand-aunt dying for me, like a talisman, in the war,
before I had even gone to Borneo
her blood vessels rushed to the surface
and burst like rockets over the wrinkled
invasion of the Australians, her eyes aslant
like the invaded, but blue like mine.
An atmosphere of supreme lucidity,
                              humanism,
the mere existence of emphasis,
                         a rusted barge
painted orange against the sea
full of Marines reciting the Arabian ideas
which are a proof in themselves of seasickness
which is a proof in itself of being hunted.
A hit? *ergo* swim.
              My 10   my 19,
my 9,   and the several years. My
12 years since they all died, philosophically speaking.
And now the coolness of a mind
like a shuttered suite in the Grand Hotel
where mail arrives for my incognito,
                         whose façade
has been slipping into the Grand Canal for centuries;
rockets splay over a *sposalizio*,
                    fleeing into night
from their Chinese memories, and it is a celebration,
the trying desperately to count them as they die.
But who will stay to be these numbers
when all the lights are dead?

43

3

The most arid stretch is often richest,
the hand lifting towards a fig tree from hunger
                                              digging
and there is water, clear, supple, or there
deep in the sand where death sleeps, a murmurous bubbling
proclaims the blackness that will ease and burn.
You preferred the Arabs? but they didn't stay to count
their inventions, racing into sands, converting themselves into
so many,
          embracing, at Ramadan, the tenderest effigies of
themselves with penises shorn by the hundreds, like a camel
ravishing a goat.   And the mountainous-minded Greeks could speak
of time as a river and step across it into Persia, leaving the pain
at home to be converted into statuary. I adore the Roman copies.
And the stench of the camel's spit I swallow,
and the stench of the whole goat. For we have advanced, France,
together into a new land, like the Greeks, where one feels nostalgic
for mere ideas, where truth lies on its deathbed like an uncle
and one of me has a sentimental longing for number,
as has another for the ball gowns of the Directoire and yet
another for "Destiny, Paris, destiny!"
                       or "Only a king may kill a king."

How many selves are there in a war hero asleep in names? under
a blanket of platoon and fleet, orderly. For every seaman
with one eye closed in fear and twitching arm at a sigh for Lord Nelson,
he is all dead; and now a meek subaltern writhes in his bedclothes
with the fury of a thousand, violating an insane mistress
who has only herself to offer his multitudes.
                                              Rising,
he wraps himself in the burnoose of memories against the heat of life
and over the sands he goes to take an algebraic position *in re*
a sun of fear shining not too bravely. He will ask himselves to
vote on fear before he feels a tremor,
                              as runners arrive from the mountains
bearing snow, proof that the mind's obsolescence is still capable
of intimacy. His mistress will follow him across the desert
like a goat, towards a mirage which is something familiar about
one of his innumerable wrists,
                              and lying in an oasis one day,
playing catch with coconuts, they suddenly smell oil.

4

Beneath these lives
the ardent lover of history hides,
                              tongue out
leaving a globe of spit on a taut spear of grass
and leaves off rattling his tail a moment
to admire this flag.
                    I'm looking for my Shanghai Lil.
Five years ago, enamored of fire-escapes, I went to Chicago,
an eventful trip: the fountains! the Art Institute, the Y
for both sexes, absent Christianity.
                                    At 7, before Jane
was up, the copper lake stirred against the sides
of a Norwegian freighter; on the deck a few dirty men,
tired of night, watched themselves in the water
as years before the German prisoners on the *Prinz Eugen*
dappled the Pacific with their sores, painted purple
by a Naval doctor.
                  Beards growing, and the constant anxiety
over looks. I'll shave before she wakes up. Sam Goldwyn
spent $2,000,000 on Anna Sten, but Grushenka left America.
One of me is standing in the waves, an ocean bather,
or I am naked with a plate of devils at my hip.
                                                Grace
to be born and live as variously as possible. The conception
of the masque barely suggests the sordid identifications.
I am a Hittite in love with a horse. I don't know what blood's
in me I feel like an African prince I am a girl walking downstairs
in a red pleated dress with heels I am a champion taking a fall
I am a jockey with a sprained ass-hole I am the light mist
                              in which a face appears
and it is another face of blonde I am a baboon eating a banana
I am a dictator looking at his wife I am a doctor eating a child
and the child's mother smiling I am a Chinaman climbing a mountain
I am a child smelling his father's underwear I am an Indian
sleeping on a scalp
                   and my pony is stamping in the birches,
and I've just caught sight of the *Niña*, the *Pinta* and the *Santa Maria*.
                    What land is this, so free?
                                              I watch
the sea at the back of my eyes, near the spot where I think
in solitude as pine trees groan and support the enormous winds,
they are humming *L'Oiseau de feu!*

45

>   They look like gods, these whitemen,
> and they are bringing me the horse I fell in love with on the frieze.

5

And now it is the serpent's turn.
I am not quite you, but almost, the opposite of visionary.
You are coiled around the central figure,
>   the heart
that bubbles with red ghosts, since to move is to love
and the scrutiny of all things is syllogistic,
the startled eyes of the dikdik, the bush full of white flags
fleeing a hunter,
>   which is our democracy
>   but the prey
is always fragile and like something, as a seashell can be
a great Courbet, if it wishes. To bend the ear of the outer world.

>   When you turn your head
can you feel your heels, undulating? that's what it is
to be a serpent. I haven't told you of the most beautiful things
in my lives, and watching the ripple of their loss disappear
along the shore, underneath ferns,
>   face downward in the ferns
my body, the naked host to my many selves, shot
by a guerrilla warrior or dumped from a car into ferns
which are themselves *journalières*.
>   The hero, trying to unhitch his parachute,
stumbles over me. It is our last embrace.
>   And yet
I have forgotten my loves, and chiefly that one, the cancerous
statue which my body could no longer contain,
>   against my will
>   against my love
become art,
>   I could not change it into history
and so remember it,
>   and I have lost what is always and everywhere
present, the scene of my selves, the occasion of these ruses,
which I myself and singly must now kill
>   and save the serpent in their midst.

A Step Away from Them

It's my lunch hour, so I go
for a walk among the hum-colored
cabs. First, down the sidewalk
where laborers feed their dirty
glistening torsos sandwiches
and Coca-Cola, with yellow helmets
on. They protect them from falling
bricks, I guess. Then onto the
avenue where skirts are flipping
above heels and blow up over
grates. The sun is hot, but the
cabs stir up the air. I look
at bargains in wristwatches. There
are cats playing in sawdust.
       On
to Times Square, where the sign
blows smoke over my head, and higher
the waterfall pours lightly. A
Negro stands in a doorway with a
toothpick, languorously agitating.
A blonde chorus girl clicks: he
smiles and rubs his chin. Everything
suddenly honks: it is 12:40 of
a Thursday.
     Neon in daylight is a
great pleasure, as Edwin Denby would
write, as are light bulbs in daylight.
I stop for a cheeseburger at JULIET'S
CORNER. Guilietta Masina, wife of
Federico Fellini, è bell' attrice.
And chocolate malted. A lady in
foxes on such a day puts her poodle
in a cab.
    There are several Puerto
Ricans on the avenue today, which
makes it beautiful and warm. First
Bunny died, then John Latouche,
then Jackson Pollock. But is the
earth as full as life was full, of them?
And one has eaten and one walks,

past the magazines with nudes
and the posters for BULLFIGHT and
the Manhattan Storage Warehouse,
which they'll soon tear down. I
used to think they had the Armory
Show there.
                A glass of papaya juice
and back to work. My heart is in my
pocket, it is Poems by Pierre Reverdy.

[It seems far away and gentle now]

It seems far away and gentle now
the morning miseries of childhood
and its raining calms over the schools

Alterable noons of loitering
beside puddles watching leaves swim
and reflected dreams of blue travels

To be always in vigilance away
from the bully who broke my nose
and so I had to break his wristwatch

A surprising violence in the sky
inspired me to my first public act
nubile and pretentious but growing pure

as the whitecaps are the wind's
but a surface agitation of the waters
means a rampart on the ocean floor is falling

And will soon be open to the tender
governing tides of a reigning will
while alterable noon assumes its virtue

Why I Am Not a Painter

I am not a painter, I am a poet.
Why? I think I would rather be
a painter, but I am not. Well,

for instance, Mike Goldberg
is starting a painting. I drop in.
"Sit down and have a drink" he
says. I drink; we drink. I look
up. "You have SARDINES in it."
"Yes, it needed something there."
"Oh." I go and the days go by
and I drop in again. The painting
is going on, and I go, and the days
go by. I drop in. The painting is
finished. "Where's SARDINES?"
All that's left is just
letters, "It was too much," Mike says.

But me? One day I am thinking of
a color: orange. I write a line
about orange. Pretty soon it is a
whole page of words, not lines.
Then another page. There should be
so much more, not of orange, of
words, of how terrible orange is
and life. Days go by. It is even in
prose, I am a real poet. My poem
is finished and I haven't mentioned
orange yet. It's twelve poems, I call
it ORANGES. And one day in a gallery
I see Mike's painting, called SARDINES.

Poem Read at Joan Mitchell's

At last you are tired of being single
the effort to be new does not upset you nor the effort to be other
you are not tired of life together

city noises are louder because you are together
being together you are louder than calling separately across a tele-
        phone one to the other
and there is no noise like the rare silence when you both sleep
even country noises—a dog bays at the moon, but when it loves the
        moon it bows, and the hitherto frowning moon fawns and slips

Only you in New York are not boring tonight
it is most modern to affirm some one
(we don't really love ideas, do we?)
and Joan was surprising you with a party for which I was the decoy
but you were surprising us by getting married and going away
so I am here reading poetry anyway
and no one will be bored tonight by me because you're here

Yesterday I felt very tired from being at the FIVE SPOT
and today I felt very tired from going to bed early and reading ULYSSES
but tonight I feel energetic because I'm sort of the bugle,
like waking people up, of your peculiar desire to get married

It's so
original, hydrogenic, anthropomorphic, fiscal, post-anti-esthetic,
        bland, unpicturesque and WilliamCarlosWilliamsian!
it's definitely not 19th Century, it's not even Partisan Review, it's
        new, it must be vanguard!

Tonight you probably walked over here from Bethune Street
down Greenwich Avenue with its sneaky little bars and the Women's De-
        tention House,
across 8th Street, by the acres of books and pillows and shoes and
        illuminating lampshades,
past Cooper Union where we heard the piece by Mortie Feldman with
        "The Stars and Stripes Forever" in it
and the Sagamore's terrific "coffee and, Andy," meaning "with a cheese
        Danish"—

did you spit on your index fingers and rub the CEDAR's neon circle for
        luck?
did you give a kind thought, hurrying, to Alger Hiss?

It's the day before February 17th
it is not snowing yet but it is dark and may snow yet
dreary February of the exhaustion from parties and the exceptional de-
        sire for spring which the ballet alone, by extending its run,
        has made bearable, dear New York City Ballet company, you are
        quite a bit like a wedding yourself!
and the only signs of spring are Maria Tallchief's rhinestones and a
        perky little dog barking in a bar, here and there eyes which
        suddenly light up with blue, like a ripple subsiding under a
        lily pad, or with brown, like a freshly plowed field we vow
        we'll drive out and look at when a certain Sunday comes in May—
and these eyes are undoubtedly Jane's and Joe's because they are ad-
        vancing into spring before us and tomorrow is Sunday

This poem goes on too long because our friendship has been long, long
        for this life and these times, long as art is long and un-
        interruptable,
and I would make it as long as I hope our friendship lasts if I could
        make poems that long

I hope there will be more
more drives to Bear Mountain and searches for hamburgers, more evenings
        avoiding the latest Japanese movie and watching Helen Vinson
        and Warner Baxter in *Vogues of 1938* instead, more discussions
        in lobbies of the respective greatnesses of Diana Adams and
        Allegra Kent,
more sunburns and more half-mile swims in which Joe beats me as Jane
        watches, lotion-covered and sleepy, more arguments over
        Faulkner's inferiority to Tolstoy while sand gets into my
        bathing trunks
let's advance and change everything, but leave these little oases in
        case the heart gets thirsty en route
and I should probably propose myself as a godfather if you have any
        children, since I will probably earn more money some day
        accidentally, and could teach him or her how to swim
and now there is a Glazunov symphony on the radio and I think of our
        friends who are not here, of John and the nuptial quality
        of his verses (he is always marrying the whole world) and

>   Janice and Kenneth, smiling and laughing, respectively (they
>   are probably laughing at the Leaning Tower right now)
> but we are all here and have their proxy
> if Kenneth were writing this he would point out how art has changed
>   women and women have changed art and men, but men haven't
>   changed women much
> but ideas are obscure and nothing should be obscure tonight
> you will live half the year in a house by the sea and half the year in
>   a house in our arms
> we peer into the future and see you happy and hope it is a sign that we
>   will be happy too, something to cling to, happiness
> the least and best of human attainments

John Button Birthday

Sentiments are nice, "The Lonely Crowd,"
a rift in the clouds appears above the purple,
you find a birthday greeting card with violets
which says "a perfect friend" and means
"I love you" but the customer is forced to be
shy. It says less, as all things must.

                                             But
grease sticks to the red ribs shaped like a
sea shell, grease, light and rosy that smells of
sandalwood: it's memory! I remember JA
staggering over to me in the San Remo and murmuring
"I've met someone MARVELLOUS!" That's friendship
for you, and the sentiment of introduction.

And now that I have finished dinner I can continue.

What is it that attracts one to one? Mystery?
I think of you in Paris with a red beard, a
theological student; in London talking to a friend
who lunched with Dowager Queen Mary and offered
her his last cigarette; in Los Angeles shopping
at the Supermarket; on Mount Shasta, looking . . .
above all on Mount Shasta in your unknown youth
and photograph.   And then the way you straighten
people out. How ambitious you are! And that you're
a painter is a great satisfaction, too. You know how
I feel about painters. I sometimes think poetry
only describes.   Now I have taken down the underwear
I washed last night from the various light fixtures
and can proceed.

                     And the lift of our experiences
together, which seem to me legendary. The long subways
to our old neighborhood the near East 49th and 53rd,
and before them the laughing in bars till we cried,
and the crying in movies till we laughed, the tenting
tonight on the old camp grounds! How beautiful it is

to visit someone for instant coffee! and you visiting
Cambridge, Massachusetts, talking for two weeks worth
in hours, and watching Maria Tallchief in the Public
Gardens while the swan-boats slumbered. And now,
not that I'm interrupting again, I mean your now,
you are 82 and I am 03. And in 1984 I trust we'll still
be high together. I'll say "Let's go to a bar"
and you'll say "Let's go to a movie" and we'll go to both;
like two old Chinese drunkards arguing about their
favorite mountain and the million reasons for them both.

Anxiety

I'm having a real day of it.
                         There was
something I had to do. But what?
There are no alternatives, just
the one something.
                    I have a drink,
it doesn't help—far from it!
                              I
feel worse. I can't remember how
I felt, so perhaps I feel better.
No. Just a little darker.
                         If I could
get really dark, richly dark, like
being drunk, that's the best that's
open as a field. Not the best,

but the best except for the impossible
pure light, to be as if above a vast
prairie, rushing and pausing over
the tiny golden heads in deep grass.

But still now, familiar laughter low
from a dark face, affection human and often even—
motivational? the warm walking night
                                    wandering
amusement of darkness, lips,
                           and
the light, always in wind. Perhaps
that's it: to clean something. A window?

Ode on Causality

> There is the sense of neurotic coherence
>
> you think maybe poetry is too important and you like that
>
> suddenly everyone's supposed to be veined, like marble
>
> it isn't that simple but it's simple enough
>
> the rock is least living of the forms man has fucked
>
> and it isn't pathetic and it's lasting, one towering tree
>
> in the vast smile of bronze and vertiginous grasses

Maude lays down her doll, red wagon and her turtle
takes my hand and comes with us, shows the bronze JACKSON POLLOCK
gazelling on the rock of her demeanor as a child, says running
away hand in hand "he isn't under there, he's out in the woods" beyond

and like that child at your grave make me be distant and imaginative
make my lines thin as ice, then swell like pythons
the color of Aurora when she first brought fire to the Arctic in a sled
a sexual bliss inscribe upon the page of whatever energy I burn for art
and do not watch over my life, but read and read through copper earth

not to fall at all, but disappear or burn! seizing a grave by throat
which is the look of earth, its ambiguity of light and sound
the thickness in a look of lust, the air within the eye
the gasp of a moving hand as maps change and faces become vacant
it's noble to refuse to be added up or divided, finality of kings

        and there's the ugliness we seek in vain
through life and long for like a mortuarian Baudelaire working for Skouras
inhabiting neighborhoods of Lear! Lear! Lear!
                                tenement of a single heart

for Old Romance was draping dolors on a scarlet mound, each face
a country of valorous decay, heath-helmet or casque, *mollement, moelleusement*
and all that shining fierce turned green and covered the lays with grass
as later in *The Orange Ballad of Cromwell's Charm Upon the Height "So Green"*
as in the histories of that same time and earlier, when written down at all
sweet scripts to obfuscate the tender subjects of their future lays

to be layed at all! romanticized, elaborated, fucked, sung, put to "rest"
is worse than the mild apprehension of a Buddhist type caught halfway up
the tea-rose trellis with his sickle banging on the Monk's lead window, moon
not our moon
         unless the tea exude a little gas and poisonous fact
to reach the spleen and give it a dreamless twinge that love love's near

    the bang of alertness, loneliness, position that prehends experience

not much to be less, not much to be more
                                alive, sick; and dead, dying
like the kiss of love meeting the kiss of hatred
                                "oh you know why"
each in asserting beginning to be more of the opposite
                                what goes up must
come down, what dooms must do, standing still and walking in New York

let us walk in that nearby forest, staring into the growling trees
in which an era of pompous frivolity or two is dangling its knobby knees
and reaching for an audience
                          over the pillar of our deaths a cloud
heaves
    pushed, steaming and blasted
                                love-propelled and tangled glitteringly
        has earned himself the title *Bird in Flight*

A True Account of Talking to the Sun at Fire Island

The Sun woke me this morning loud
and clear, saying "Hey! I've been
trying to wake you up for fifteen
minutes. Don't be so rude, you are
only the second poet I've ever chosen
to speak to personally
                            so why
aren't you more attentive? If I could
burn you through the window I would
to wake you up. I can't hang around
here all day."
               "Sorry, Sun, I stayed
up late last night talking to Hal."

"When I woke up Mayakovsky he was
a lot more prompt" the Sun said
petulantly. "Most people are up
already waiting to see if I'm going
to put in an appearance."
                        I tried
to apologize "I missed you yesterday."
"That's better" he said. "I didn't
know you'd come out." "You may be
wondering why I've come so close?"
"Yes" I said beginning to feel hot
wondering if maybe he wasn't burning me
anyway.
          "Frankly I wanted to tell you
I like your poetry. I see a lot
on my rounds and you're okay. You may
not be the greatest thing on earth, but
you're different. Now, I've heard some
say you're crazy, they being excessively
calm themselves to my mind, and other
crazy poets think that you're a boring
reactionary. Not me.
                Just keep on
like I do and pay no attention. You'll
find that people always will complain

about the atmosphere, either too hot
or too cold too bright or too dark, days
too short or too long.
                         If you don't appear
at all one day they think you're lazy
or dead. Just keep right on, I like it.

And don't worry about your lineage
poetic or natural. The Sun shines on
the jungle, you know, on the tundra
the sea, the ghetto. Wherever you were
I knew it and saw you moving. I was waiting
for you to get to work.

                         And now that you
are making your own days, so to speak,
even if no one reads you but me
you won't be depressed. Not
everyone can look up, even at me. It
hurts their eyes."
                 "Oh Sun, I'm so grateful to you!"

"Thanks and remember I'm watching. It's
easier for me to speak to you out
here. I don't have to slide down
between buildings to get your ear.
I know you love Manhattan, but
you ought to look up more often.
                                 And
always embrace things, people earth
sky stars, as I do, freely and with
the appropriate sense of space. That
is your inclination, known in the heavens
and you should follow it to hell, if
necessary, which I doubt.
                         Maybe we'll
speak again in Africa, of which I too
am specially fond. Go back to sleep now
Frank, and I may leave a tiny poem
in that brain of yours as my farewell."

"Sun, don't go!" I was awake at last. "No, go I must, they're calling me."

"Who are they?"

Rising he said "Some day you'll know. They're calling to you too." Darkly he rose, and then I slept.

To Gottfried Benn

Poetry is not instruments
that work at times
then walk out on you
laugh at you old
get drunk on you young
poetry's part of your self

like the passion of a nation
at war it moves quickly
provoked to defense or aggression
unreasoning power
an instinct for self-declaration

like nations its faults are absorbed
in the heat of sides and angles
combatting the void of rounds
a solid of imperfect placement
nations get worse and worse

but not wrongly revealed
in the universal light of tragedy

The Day Lady Died

It is 12:20 in New York a Friday
three days after Bastille day, yes
it is 1959 and I go get a shoeshine
because I will get off the 4:19 in Easthampton
at 7:15 and then go straight to dinner
and I don't know the people who will feed me

I walk up the muggy street beginning to sun
and have a hamburger and a malted and buy
an ugly NEW WORLD WRITING to see what the poets
in Ghana are doing these days
                                      I go on to the bank
and Miss Stillwagon (first name Linda I once heard)
doesn't even look up my balance for once in her life
and in the GOLDEN GRIFFIN I get a little Verlaine
for Patsy with drawings by Bonnard although I do
think of Hesiod, trans. Richmond Lattimore or
Brendan Behan's new play or *Le Balcon* or *Les Nègres*
of Genet, but I don't, I stick with Verlaine
after practically going to sleep with quandariness

and for Mike I just stroll into the PARK LANE
Liquor Store and ask for a bottle of Strega and
then I go back where I came from to 6th Avenue
and the tobacconist in the Ziegfeld Theatre and
casually ask for a carton of Gauloises and a carton
of Picayunes, and a NEW YORK POST with her face on it

and I am sweating a lot by now and thinking of
leaning on the john door in the 5 SPOT
while she whispered a song along the keyboard
to Mal Waldron and everyone and I stopped breathing

Adieu to Norman,
Bon Jour to Joan and Jean-Paul

It is 12:10 in New York and I am wondering
if I will finish this in time to meet Norman for lunch
ah lunch! I think I am going crazy
what with my terrible hangover and the weekend coming up
at excitement-prone Kenneth Koch's
I wish I were staying in town and working on my poems
at Joan's studio for a new book by Grove Press
which they will probably not print
but it is good to be several floors up in the dead of night
wondering whether you are any good or not
and the only decision you can make is that you did it

yesterday I looked up the rue Frémicourt on a map
and was happy to find it like a bird
flying over Paris et ses environs
which unfortunately did not include Seine-et-Oise which I don't know
as well as a number of other things
and Allen is back talking about god a lot
and Peter is back not talking very much
and Joe has a cold and is not coming to Kenneth's
although he is coming to lunch with Norman
I suspect he is making a distinction
well, who isn't

I wish I were reeling around Paris
instead of reeling around New York
I wish I weren't reeling at all
it is Spring the ice has melted the Ricard is being poured
we are all happy and young and toothless
it is the same as old age
the only thing to do is simply continue
is that simple
yes, it is simple because it is the only thing to do
can you do it
yes, you can because it is the only thing to do
blue light over the Bois de Boulogne it continues
the Seine continues
the Louvre stays open it continues it hardly closes at all
the Bar Américain continues to be French

de Gaulle continues to be Algerian as does Camus
Shirley Goldfarb continues to be Shirley Goldfarb
and Jane Hazan continues to be Jane Freilicher (I think!)
and Irving Sandler continues to be the balayeur des artistes
and so do I (sometimes I think I'm "in love" with painting)
and surely the Piscine Deligny continues to have water in it
and the Flore continues to have tables and newspapers and people under them
and surely we shall not continue to be unhappy
we shall be happy
but we shall continue to be ourselves everything continues to be possible
René Char, Pierre Reverdy, Samuel Beckett it is possible isn't it
I love Reverdy for saying yes, though I don't believe it

Joe's Jacket

Entraining to Southampton in the parlor car with Jap and Vincent, I
see life as a penetrable landscape lit from above
like it was in my Barbizonian kiddy days when automobiles
were owned by the same people for years and the Alfa Romeo was
only a rumor under the leaves beside the viaduct and I
pretending to be adult felt the blue within me and the light up there
no central figure me, I was some sort of cloud or a gust of wind
at the station a crowd of drunken fishermen on a picnic Kenneth
is hard to find but we find, through all the singing, Kenneth smiling
it is off to Janice's bluefish and the incessant talk of affection
expressed as excitability and spleen to be recent and strong
and not unbearably right in attitude, full of confidences
now I will say it, thank god, I knew you would

an enormous party mesmerizing comers in the disgathering light
and dancing miniature-endless like a pivot
I drink to smother my sensitivity for a while so I won't stare away
I drink to kill the fear of boredom, the mounting panic of it
I drink to reduce my seriousness so a certain spurious charm
can appear and win its flickering little victory over noise
I drink to die a little and increase the contrast of this questionable moment
and then I am going home, purged of everything except anxiety and self-distrust
now I will say it, thank god, I knew you would
and the rain has commenced its delicate lament over the orchards

an enormous window morning and the wind, the beautiful desperation of a tree
fighting off strangulation, and my bed has an ugly calm
I reach to the D.H. Lawrence on the floor and read "The Ship of Death"
I lie back again and begin slowly to drift and then to sink
a somnolent envy of inertia makes me rise naked and go to the window
where the car horn mysteriously starts to honk, no one is there
and Kenneth comes out and stops it in the soft green lightless stare
and we are soon in the Paris of Kenneth's libretto, I did not drift
away I did not die I am there with Haussmann and the rue de Rivoli
and the spirits of beauty, art and progress, pertinent and mobile
in their worldly way, and musical and strange the sun comes out

returning by car the forceful histories of myself and Vincent loom
like the city hour after hour closer and closer to the future I am here
and the night is heavy though not warm, Joe is still up and we talk
only of the immediate present and its indiscriminately hitched-to past
the feeling of life and incident pouring over the sleeping city
which seems to be bathed in an unobtrusive light which lends things
coherence and an absolute, for just that time as four o'clock goes by

and soon I am rising for the less than average day, I have coffee
I prepare calmly to face almost everything that will come up I am calm
but not as my bed was calm as it softly declined to become a ship
I borrow Joe's seersucker jacket though he is still asleep I start out
when I last borrowed it I was leaving there it was on my Spanish plaza back
and hid my shoulders from San Marco's pigeons was jostled on the Kurfürstendamm
and sat opposite Ashes in an enormous leather chair in the Continental
it is all enormity and life it has protected me and kept me here on
many occasions as a symbol does when the heart is full and risks no speech
a precaution I loathe as the pheasant loathes the season and is preserved
it will not be need, it will be just what it is and just what happens

You Are Gorgeous and I'm Coming

Vaguely I hear the purple roar of the torn-down Third Avenue El
it sways slightly but firmly like a hand or a golden-downed thigh
normally I don't think of sounds as colored unless I'm feeling corrupt
concrete Rimbaud obscurity of emotion which is simple and very definite
even lasting, yes it may be that dark and purifying wave, the death of boredom
nearing the heights themselves may destroy you in the pure air
to be further complicated, confused, empty but refilling, exposed to light

With the past falling away as an acceleration of nerves thundering and shaking
aims its aggregating force like the Métro towards a realm of encircling travel
rending the sound of adventure and becoming ultimately local and intimate
repeating the phrases of an old romance which is constantly renewed by the
endless originality of human loss the air the stumbling quiet of breathing
newly the heavens' stars all out we are all for the captured time of our being

Poem

Hate is only one of many responses
true, hurt and hate go hand in hand
but why be afraid of hate, it is only there

think of filth, is it really awesome
neither is hate
don't be shy of unkindness, either
it's cleansing and allows you to be direct
like an arrow that feels something

out and out meanness, too, lets love breathe
you don't have to fight off getting in too deep
you can always get out if you're not too scared

an ounce of prevention's
enough to poison the heart
don't think of others
until you have thought of yourself, are true

all of these things, if you feel them
will be graced by a certain reluctance
and turn into gold

if felt by me, will be smilingly deflected
by your mysterious concern

Personal Poem

Now when I walk around at lunchtime
I have only two charms in my pocket
an old Roman coin Mike Kanemitsu gave me
and a bolt-head that broke off a packing case
when I was in Madrid the others never
brought me too much luck though they did
help keep me in New York against coercion
but now I'm happy for a time and interested

I walk through the luminous humidity
passing the House of Seagram with its wet
and its loungers and the construction to
the left that closed the sidewalk if
I ever get to be a construction worker
I'd like to have a silver hat please
and get to Moriarty's where I wait for
LeRoi and hear who wants to be a mover and
shaker the last five years my batting average
is .016 that's that, and LeRoi comes in
and tells me Miles Davis was clubbed 12
times last night outside BIRDLAND by a cop
a lady asks us for a nickel for a terrible
disease but we don't give her one we
don't like terrible diseases, then
we go eat some fish and some ale it's
cool but crowded we don't like Lionel Trilling
we decide, we like Don Allen we don't like
Henry James so much we like Herman Melville
we don't want to be in the poets' walk in
San Francisco even we just want to be rich
and walk on girders in our silver hats
I wonder if one person out of the 8,000,000 is
thinking of me as I shake hands with LeRoi
and buy a strap for my wristwatch and go
back to work happy at the thought possibly so

Post the Lake Poets Ballad

Moving slowly sweating a lot
I am pushed by a gentle breeze
outside the Paradise Bar on
      St. Mark's Place and I breathe

and bourbon with Joe he says
did you see a letter from Larry
in the mailbox what a shame I didn't
      I wonder what it says

and then we eat and go to
The Horse Riders and my bum aches
from the hard seats and boredom
      is hard too we don't go

to the Cedar it's so hot out
and I read the letter which says
in your poems your gorgeous self-pity
      how do you like that

that is odd I think of myself
as a cheerful type who pretends to
be hurt to get a little depth into
      things that interest me

and I've even given that up
lately with the stream of events
going so fast and the movingly
      alternating with the amusingly

the depth all in the ocean
although I'm different in the winter
of course even this is a complaint
      but I'm happy anyhow

no more self-pity than Gertrude
Stein before Lucey Church or Savonarola
in the pulpit Allen Ginsberg at the
      Soviet Exposition am I Joe

Poem

Khrushchev is coming on the right day!
                              the cool graced light
is pushed off the enormous glass piers by hard wind
and everything is tossing, hurrying on up
                              this country
has everything but *politesse*, a Puerto Rican cab driver says
and five different girls I see
                    look like Piedie Gimbel
with her blonde hair tossing too,
                    as she looked when I pushed
her little daughter on the swing on the lawn it was also windy

last night we went to a movie and came out,
                              Ionesco is greater
than Beckett, Vincent said, that's what I think, blueberry blintzes
and Khrushchev was probably being carped at
                    in Washington, no *politesse*
Vincent tells me about his mother's trip to Sweden
                              Hans tells us
about his father's life in Sweden, it sounds like Grace Hartigan's
painting *Sweden*
          so I go home to bed and names drift through my head
Purgatorio Merchado, Gerhard Schwartz and Gaspar Gonzales, all
          unknown figures of the early morning as I go to work

where does the evil of the year go
                    when September takes New York
and turns it into ozone stalagmites
                         deposits of light
                         so I get back up
make coffee, and read François Villon, his life, so dark
    New York seems blinding and my tie is blowing up the street
I wish it would blow off
              though it is cold and somewhat warms my neck
as the train bears Khrushchev on to Pennsylvania Station
    and the light seems to be eternal
    and joy seems to be inexorable
    I am foolish enough always to find it in wind

Getting Up Ahead of Someone (Sun)

I cough a lot (sinus?) so I
get up and have some tea with cognac
it is dawn
           the light flows evenly along the lawn
in chilly Southampton and I smoke
and hours and hours go by I read
van Vechten's *Spider Boy* then a short
story by Patsy Southgate and a poem
by myself it is cold and I shiver a little
in white shorts the day begun
so oddly not tired not nervous I
am for once truly awake letting it all
start slowly as I watch instead of
grabbing on late as usual
                      where did it go
                      it's not really awake yet
                      I will wait

and the house wakes up and goes
to get the dog in Sag Harbor I make
myself a bourbon and commence
to write one of my "I do this I do that"
poems in a sketch pad
                  it is tomorrow
though only six hours have gone by
each day's light has more significance these days

Hôtel Transylvanie

Shall we win at love or shall we lose
                              can it be
that hurting and being hurt is a trick forcing the love
we want to appear, that the hurt is a card
and is it black? is it red? is it a paper, dry of tears
chevalier, change your expression! the wind is sweeping over
the gaming tables ruffling the cards/they are black and red
like a Futurist torture and how do you know it isn't always there
waiting while doubt is the father that has you kidnapped by friends

     yet you will always live in a jealous society of accident
you will never know how beautiful you are or how beautiful
the other is, you will continue to refuse to die for yourself
you will continue to sing on trying to cheer everyone up
and they will know as they listen with excessive pleasure that you're dead
     and they will not mind that they have let you entertain
at the expense of the only thing you want in the world/you are amusing
as a game is amusing when someone is forced to lose as in a game I must

          oh *hôtel*, you should be merely a bed
surrounded by walls where two souls meet and do nothing but breathe
breathe in breathe out fuse illuminate confuse *stick* dissemble
but not as cheaters at cards have something to win/you have only to be
as you are being, as you must be, as you always are, as you shall be forever
no matter what fate deals you or the imagination discards like a tyrant
as the drums descend and summon the hatchet over the tinselled realities

you know that I am not here to fool around, that I must win or die
I expect you to do everything because it is of no consequence/no duel
you must rig the deck you must make me win at whatever cost to the reputation
of the establishment/sublime moment of dishonest hope/I must win
for if the floods of tears arrive they will wash it all away
                                                                          and then
you will know what it is to want something, but you may not be allowed
to die as I have died, you may only be allowed to drift downstream
to another body of inimical attractions for which you will substitute/distrust
and I will have had my revenge on the black bitch of my nature which you
                              love as I have never loved myself

but I hold on/I am lyrical to a fault/I do not despair being too foolish
where will you find me, projective verse, since I will be gone?
for six seconds of your beautiful face I will sell the hotel and commit
an uninteresting suicide in Louisiana where it will take them a long time
to know who I am/why I came there/what and why I am and made to happen

Poem

That's not a cross look it's a sign of life
but I'm glad you care how I look at you
this morning (after I got up) I was thinking
of President Warren G. Harding and Horace S.
Warren, father of the little blonde girl
across the street and another blonde Agnes
Hedlund (this was in the 6th grade)   what

now the day has begun in a soft grey way
with elephantine traffic trudging along Fifth
and two packages of Camels in my pocket
I can't think of one interesting thing Warren
G. Harding did, I guess I was passing notes
to Sally and Agnes at the time he came up
in our elephantine history course everything

seems slow suddenly and boring except
for my insatiable thinking towards you
as you lie asleep completely plotzed and
gracious as a hillock in the mist from one
small window, sunless and only slightly open
as is your mouth and presently your quiet eyes
your breathing is like that history lesson

Avenue A

We hardly ever see the moon any more
                              so no wonder
    it's so beautiful when we look up suddenly
and there it is gliding broken-faced over the bridges
brilliantly coursing, soft, and a cool wind fans
         your hair over your forehead and your memories
              of Red Grooms' locomotive landscape
I want some bourbon/you want some oranges/I love the leather
              jacket Norman gave me
                              and the corduroy coat David
    gave you, it is more mysterious than spring, the El Greco
heavens breaking open and then reassembling like lions
                         in a vast tragic veldt
    that is far from our small selves and our temporally united
passions in the cathedral of Januaries

         everything is too comprehensible
these are my delicate and caressing poems
I suppose there will be more of those others to come, as in the past
                        so many
but for now the moon is revealing itself like a pearl
                         to my equally naked heart

Steps

How funny you are today New York
like Ginger Rogers in *Swingtime*
and St. Bridget's steeple leaning a little to the left

here I have just jumped out of a bed full of V-days
(I got tired of D-days) and blue you there still
accepts me foolish and free
all I want is a room up there
and you in it
and even the traffic halt so thick is a way
for people to rub up against each other
and when their surgical appliances lock
they stay together
for the rest of the day (what a day)
I go by to check a slide and I say
that painting's not so blue

where's Lana Turner
she's out eating
and Garbo's backstage at the Met
everyone's taking their coat off
so they can show a rib-cage to the rib-watchers
and the park's full of dancers with their tights and shoes
in little bags
who are often mistaken for worker-outers at the West Side Y
why not
the Pittsburgh Pirates shout because they won
and in a sense we're all winning
we're alive

the apartment was vacated by a gay couple
who moved to the country for fun
they moved a day too soon
even the stabbings are helping the population explosion
though in the wrong country
and all those liars have left the UN
the Seagram Building's no longer rivalled in interest
not that we need liquor (we just like it)

and the little box is out on the sidewalk
next to the delicatessen
so the old man can sit on it and drink beer
and get knocked off it by his wife later in the day
while the sun is still shining

oh god it's wonderful
to get out of bed
and drink too much coffee
and smoke too many cigarettes
and love you so much

Ave Maria

Mothers of America
                       let your kids go to the movies!
get them out of the house so they won't know what you're up to
it's true that fresh air is good for the body
                                    but what about the soul
that grows in darkness, embossed by silvery images
and when you grow old as grow old you must
                                    they won't hate you
they won't criticize you they won't know
                                they'll be in some glamorous country
they first saw on a Saturday afternoon or playing hookey

they may even be grateful to you
                             for their first sexual experience
which only cost you a quarter
                           and didn't upset the peaceful home
they will know where candy bars come from
                                and gratuitous bags of popcorn
as gratuitous as leaving the movie before it's over
with a pleasant stranger whose apartment is in the Heaven on Earth Bldg
near the Williamsburg Bridge
                         oh mothers you will have made the little tykes
so happy because if nobody does pick them up in the movies
they won't know the difference
                         and if somebody does it'll be sheer gravy
and they'll have been truly entertained either way
instead of hanging around the yard
                       or up in their room
                                  hating you
prematurely since you won't have done anything horribly mean yet
except keeping them from the darker joys
                            it's unforgivable the latter
so don't blame me if you won't take this advice
                             and the family breaks up
and your children grow old and blind in front of a TV set
                                     seeing
movies you wouldn't let them see when they were young

Essay on Style

Someone else's Leica sitting on the table
the black kitchen table I am painting
the floor yellow, Bill is painting it
wouldn't you know my mother would call
up
    and complain?
                    my sister's pregnant and
went to the country for the weekend without
telling her
        in point of fact why don't I
go out to have dinner with her or "let her"
come in? well if Mayor Wagner won't allow private
cars on Manhattan because of the snow, I
will probably never see her again
                          considering
my growingly more perpetual state and how
can one say that angel in the Frick's wings
are "attached" if it's a real angel? now

I was reflecting the other night meaning
I was being reflected upon that Sheridan Square
is remarkably beautiful, sitting in JACK
DELANEY's looking out the big race-track window
on the wet
        drinking a cognac while Edwin
read my new poem it occurred to me how impossible
it is to fool Edwin not that I don't know as
much as the next about obscurity in modern verse
but he
    always knows what it's about as well
as what it is do you think we can ever
strike *as* and *but*, too, out of the language
then we can attack *well* since it has no
application whatsoever neither as a state
of being or a rest for the mind no such
things available
                where do you think I've
got to? the spectacle of a grown man
decorating
        a Christmas tree disgusts me that's

where
        that's one of the places yetbutaswell
I'm glad I went to that party for Ed Dorn
last night though he didn't show up do you think
,Bill, we can get rid of *though* also, and *also*?
maybe your
           lettrism is the only answer treating
the typewriter as an intimate organ why not?
nothing else is (intimate)
                   no I am not going
to have you "in" for dinner nor am I going "out"
I am going to eat alone for the rest of my life

Poem

Lana Turner has collapsed!
I was trotting along and suddenly
it started raining and snowing
and you said it was hailing
but hailing hits you on the head
hard so it was really snowing and
raining and I was in such a hurry
to meet you but the traffic
was acting exactly like the sky
and suddenly I see a headline
LANA TURNER HAS COLLAPSED!
there is no snow in Hollywood
there is no rain in California
I have been to lots of parties
and acted perfectly disgraceful
but I never actually collapsed
oh Lana Turner we love you get up

First Dances

1

From behind he takes her waist
and lifts her, her lavender waist
stained with tears and her mascara
is running, her neck is tired
from drooping. She floats she steps
automatically correct, then suddenly
she is alive up there and smiles.
How much greater triumph for him
that she had so despaired when his
hands encircled her like a pillar
and lifted her into the air
which after him will turn to rock-
like boredom, but not till after
many hims and he will not be there.

2

The punch bowl was near the cloakroom
so the pints could be taken out of the
boys' cloaks and dumped into the punch.
Outside the branches beat hysterically
towards the chandeliers, just fended
off by fearful windows. The chandeliers
giggle a little. There were many
introductions but few invitations. I
found a spot of paint on my coat as
others found pimples. It is easy to
dance it is even easy to dance together
sometimes. We were very young and ugly
we knew it, everybody knew it.

3

A white hall inside a church. Nerves.

Walking

I get a cinder in my eye
                       it streams into
     the sunlight
               the air pushes it aside
and I drop my hot dog
                    into one of the Seagram Building's
fountains
         it is all watery and clear and windy

the shape of the toe as
                it describes the pain
of the ball of the foot,
           walking walking on
asphalt
      the strange embrace of the ankle's
lock
    on the pavement
               squared like mausoleums
but cheerful
      moved over and stamped on
slapped by winds
            the country is no good for us
there's nothing
       to bump into
                or fall apart glassily
there's not enough
          poured concrete
                and brassy
reflections
      the wind now takes me to
The Narrows
        and I see it rising there
                   New York
greater than the Rocky Mountains

Fantasy
dedicated to the health of Allen Ginsberg

How do you like the music of Adolph
                                                Deutsch? I like
it, I like it better than Max Steiner's. Take his
score for *Northern Pursuit*, the Helmut Dantine theme
was . . .
                and then the window fell on my hand. Errol
Flynn was skiing by. Down
                              down down went the grim
grey submarine under the "cold" ice.
                                      Helmut was
safely ashore, on the ice.
                         What dreams, what incredible
fantasies of snow farts will this all lead to?
                                            I
don't know, I have stopped thinking like a sled dog.

The main thing is to tell a story.
                                  It is almost
very important. Imagine
                            throwing away the avalanche
so early in the movie. I am the only spy left
in Canada,
              but just because I'm alone in the snow
doesn't necessarily mean I'm a Nazi.
                                      Let's see,
two aspirins a vitamin C tablet and some baking soda
should do the trick, that's practically an
                                          Alka
Seltzer. Allen come out of the bathroom
                                        and take it.
I think someone put butter on my skis instead
of wax.
          Ouch. The leanto is falling over in the
firs, and there is another fatter spy here. They
didn't tell me they sent
                        him. Well, that takes care
of him, boy were those huskies hungry.
                                        Allen,

are you feeling any better? Yes, I'm crazy about
Helmut Dantine
                    but I'm glad that Canada will remain
free. Just free, that's all, never argue with the movies.

Personism: A Manifesto

Everything is in the poems, but at the risk of sounding like the poor wealthy man's Allen Ginsberg I will write to you because I just heard that one of my fellow poets thinks that a poem of mine that can't be got at one reading is because I was confused too. Now, come on. I don't believe in god, so I don't have to make elaborately sounded structures. I hate Vachel Lindsay, always have; I don't even like rhythm, assonance, all that stuff. You just go on your nerve. If someone's chasing you down the street with a knife you just run, you don't turn around and shout, "Give it up! I was a track star for Mineola Prep."

That's for the writing poems part. As for their reception, suppose you're in love and someone's mistreating (*mal aimé*) you, you don't say, "Hey, you can't hurt me this way, I care!" you just let all the different bodies fall where they may, and they always do may after a few months. But that's not why you fell in love in the first place, just to hang onto life, so you have to take your chances and try to avoid being logical. Pain always produces logic, which is very bad for you.

I'm not saying that I don't have practically the most lofty ideas of anyone writing today, but what difference does that make? They're just ideas. The only good thing about it is that when I get lofty enough I've stopped thinking and that's when refreshment arrives.

But how can you really care if anybody gets it, or gets what it means, or if it improves them. Improves them for what? For death? Why hurry them along? Too many poets act like a middle-aged mother trying to get her kids to eat too much cooked meat, and potatoes with drippings (tears). I don't give a damn whether they eat or not. Forced feeding leads to excessive thinness (effete). Nobody should experience anything they don't need to, if they don't need poetry bully for them. I like the movies too. And after all, only Whitman and Crane and Williams, of the American poets are better than the movies. As for measure and other technical apparatus, that's just common sense: if you're going to buy a pair of pants you want them to be tight enough so everyone will want to go to bed with you. There's nothing metaphysical about it. Unless, of course, you flatter yourself into thinking that what you're experiencing is "yearning."

Abstraction in poetry, which Allen [Ginsberg] recently commented on in *It is*, is intriguing. I think it appears mostly in the minute particulars where decision is necessary. Abstraction (in poetry, not in painting) involves personal removal by the poet. For instance, the decision involved in the choice between "the nostalgia *of* the infinite" and "the nostalgia *for* the infinite" defines an attitude towards degree of abstraction. The nostalgia *of* the infinite representing the greater degree of abstraction, removal and negative capability (as in Keats and Mallarmé). Personism, a movement which I recently founded and which nobody knows about, interests me a great deal, being so totally opposed to this kind of abstract removal that it is verging on a true abstraction for the first time, really, in the history of poetry. Personism is to Wallace Stevens what *la poésie pure* was to Béranger. Personism has nothing to do with philosophy, it's all art. It does not have to do with personality or intimacy, far from it! But to give you a vague idea, one of its minimal aspects is to address itself to one person (other than the poet himself), thus evoking overtones of love without destroying love's life-giving vulgarity, and sustaining the poet's feelings towards the poem while preventing love from distracting him into feeling about the person. That's part of Personism. It was founded by me after lunch with LeRoi Jones on August 27, 1959, a day in which I was in love with someone (not Roi, by the way, a blond). I went back to work and wrote a poem for this person. While I was writing it I was realizing that if I wanted to I could use the telephone instead of writing the poem, and so Personism was born. It's a very exciting movement which will undoubtedly have lots of adherents. It puts the poem squarely between the poet and the person, Lucky Pierre style, and the poem is correspondingly gratified. The poem is at last between two persons instead of two pages. In all modesty, I confess that it may be the death of literature as we know it. While I have certain regrets, I am still glad I got there before Alain Robbe-Grillet did. Poetry being quicker and surer than prose, it is only just that poetry finish literature off. For a time people thought that Artaud was going to accomplish this, but actually, for all their magnificence, his polemical writings are not more outside literature than Bear Mountain is outside New York State. His relation is no more astounding than Dubuffet's to painting.

What can we expect of Personism? (This is getting good, isn't it?) Everything, but we won't get it. It is too new, too vital a movement to promise anything. But it, like Africa, is on the way. The recent propagandists for technique on the one hand, and for content on the other, had better watch out.

September 3, 1959

Select Bibliography

Poetry
A City Winter and Other Poems. New York: Tibor de Nagy Gallery, 1951
Oranges, 12 Pastorals. New York: Tibor de Nagy Gallery, 1953
Meditations in an Emergency. New York: Grove Press, 1957, 1967 / Grove/Atlantic, 1996
Second Avenue. New York: Totem Press in association with Corinth Books, 1960
Odes. New York: Tiber Press, 1961
Lunch Poems. San Francisco: City Lights Books, 1964
Love Poems (Tentative Title). New York: Tibor de Nagy Editions, 1965
In Memory of My Feelings: A Selection of Poems. Ed. Bill Berkson. New York: Museum of Modern Art, 1967
The Collected Poems of Frank O'Hara. Ed. Donald Allen. New York: Alfred A. Knopf, 1971 / Berkeley: The University of California Press, 1995
The Selected Poems of Frank O'Hara. Ed. Donald Allen. New York: Alfred A. Knopf / Vintage Books, 1974. Manchester, UK: Carcanet, 1991 / London: Penguin Books, 1994
Poems Retrieved. Ed. Donald Allen. San Francisco: Grey Fox Press, 1977, 1996
Early Writing. Ed. Donald Allen. San Francisco: Grey Fox Press, 1977
Poems with lithographs by Willem de Kooning. New York: The Limited Editions Club, 1989
Biotherm with lithographs by Jim Dine, and essay by Bill Berkson. San Francisco: Arion Press, 1990
Hymns of St. Bridget & Other Writings by Bill Berkson and Frank O'Hara. Woodacre, CA: The Owl Press, 2001

Prose
Jackson Pollock. New York: George Braziller, 1959
New Spanish Painting and Sculpture. New York: Museum of Modern Art, 1960
Nakian. New York: Museum of Modern Art, 1966
Art Chronicles 1954-1966. New York: George Braziller, 1975, 1991
Standing Still and Walking in New York. Ed. Donald Allen. San Francisco: Grey Fox Press, 1975
What's With Modern Art? Selected Short Reviews & Other Art Writings. Ed. Bill Berkson. Austin, Texas: Mike & Dale's Press, 1999

Plays
Amorous Nightmares of Delay: Selected Plays. Ed. Ron Padgett, Joan Simon, and Ann Waldman. Baltimore: Johns Hopkins University Press, 1995
First edition titled *Selected Plays*. New York: Full Court Press, 1978